GW01159290

Original title:
The Way I Feel

Author: Amelia Montgomery
ISBN HARDBACK: 978-9916-88-938-1
ISBN PAPERBACK: 978-9916-88-939-8

Labyrinth of Lingering Thoughts

In shadows deep, my mind does stray,
Through twisted paths where ideas play.
Fragmented whispers haunt each turn,
In quiet corners, candles burn.

A maze of doubts, where echoes roam,
Each thought a traveler, far from home.
Yet in this chaos, clarity glows,
A hidden truth beneath each prose.

Chasing Distant Dreams

Across the skies, my visions soar,
In twilight hues, I seek for more.
With every step, the stars align,
In whispered hopes, I find the sign.

Through valleys low and mountains steep,
I chase the dreams that dare to leap.
With open heart, I make my way,
For every dawn brings forth a ray.

Waves of Restless Longing

The ocean calls with a siren's song,
Each wave a heartbeat, deep and strong.
Restless tides pull me to the shore,
Where secrets linger, forevermore.

In moonlit nights, my heart does ache,
For distant shores, where dreams may break.
With every crest, my spirit finds,
A dance of hope that ever binds.

Portraits of Fleeting Moments

Captured smiles in time's embrace,
Moments painted, a timeless chase.
In frames of love, we find our spark,
Each snapshot glows, a vibrant mark.

The laughter shared and silent tears,
Composed of whispers, hopes, and fears.
Each portrait tells a tale so grand,
Of fleeting seconds held in hand.

Hues of Hope on the Horizon

Soft whispers of dawn begin to unfold,
Painting the sky in colors so bold.
Each stroke a promise, a dream to embrace,
As the light breaks free, filling empty space.

Golden rays dance on the morning dew,
Filling our hearts with a warmth so true.
In every shade, a story we find,
Hues of hope guiding the heart and mind.

Notes from a Weathered Soul

Rustling leaves echo tales long past,
The weight of the years, shadows are cast.
Yet in every wrinkle, wisdom takes flight,
Beneath the sorrow, a flicker of light.

Cracked pages whisper memories near,
Mingling laughter with heartache and fear.
Each note a treasure, sung soft and low,
In the symphony of life, we ebb and flow.

Wandering Through Memory's Garden

In this garden of thoughts, I wander alone,
Among fragrant blossoms, where echoes have grown.
Petals of laughter, the thorns of regret,
A tapestry woven, each moment I'll never forget.

The fragrance of youth fills the still, crisp air,
As I trace the paths to the lost and rare.
Each corner reveals a familiar face,
In memory's garden, love finds its place.

Embracing Shadows as Friends

Shadows linger softly, companions in sight,
In the twilight moments, they dance with delight.
Through the depths of despair, they whisper solace,
Teaching us courage, in quiet embrace.

With arms open wide, we welcome the night,
For in every shadow, there's also a light.
Together we face the fears that abound,
In the heart of the darkness, true strength can be found.

Bridges Built on Fleeting Moments

Whispers carried on the breeze,
Footsteps tracing paths unseen,
Hearts collide in silent ease,
Embracing all that might have been.

Moments flicker like a flame,
Each smile a fragile thread,
In the tapestry of our name,
Threads of gold for what we said.

Fleeting glances, timeless ties,
Across the chasms we have crossed,
Building bridges where love flies,
In the moments, not the lost.

Together we defy the night,
Finding home in tender grace,
With each heartbeat, pure delight,
In the fleeting, we find place.

Serendipity in the Unexpected

A chance encounter, eyes align,
Unfolding stories yet untold,
In every twist, in every line,
Mysteries of fate unfold.

A laugh escapes, a lingering glance,
Paths converge in perfect sync,
Caught in a blissful, wild dance,
Defying logic, hearts will think.

Moments wrapped in soft surprise,
Life's gentle nudges push and pull,
Hidden treasures in disguise,
Every heartbeat, beautiful.

Embracing what life will bestow,
We wander where the wild winds blow,
Serendipity's warm glow,
Guides us to where love can grow.

Lost in the Dance of Daydreams

Swirling thoughts like autumn leaves,
In the stillness, voices play,
Weaving tales that time deceives,
In daydreams, we drift away.

Fields of wonder, skies of blue,
Moments wrapped in softest light,
Every dream a journey new,
Carried by the starry night.

Floating high on whispered winds,
Imagined worlds at our command,
Each daydream, where the heart begins,
A dance of hope, a gentle hand.

Lost in thoughts, we find our way,
Through the labyrinth of our minds,
Every sigh a sweet ballet,
In daydreams, joy endlessly finds.

Underneath a Moonlit Veil

Shadows dance on silvery streams,
Whispers soft as gentle night,
Beneath the stars, we chase our dreams,
Wrapped in warmth, bathed in light.

The moon unveils a world of sighs,
Each heartbeat sparkles like a star,
In the quiet, love never lies,
Connected, no matter how far.

Dreams reflected in your eyes,
Promises stitched in twilight's seam,
Beneath the vast, embracing skies,
We wander deep within a dream.

In the night, all fears disperse,
Every heartbeat sings of love,
Underneath the moon's soft curse,
We find our way, guided above.

The Clock's Relentless Whisper

Ticking softly in the night,
Time slips by, a fleeting flight.
Moments lost and memories tight,
The clock's whisper, a fading light.

Seconds drip like falling rain,
Echoes of joy, shadows of pain.
A constant march, we feel the strain,
Yet in its rhythm, we find our gain.

Hands that move without a care,
Every heartbeat, laid out bare.
Life continues, unaware,
In the stillness, we must dare.

Timeless wisdom, softly spoken,
Every second, a promise broken.
Yet in this dance, our lives are woven,
From clock's relentless whisper, we're awoken.

A Soft Place for Reclusive Thoughts

In a garden where dreams reside,
Shadows dance and secrets hide.
A soft place where fears subside,
And whispers of the heart abide.

Petals fall like gentle sighs,
Nurturing hopes beneath the skies.
Quiet corners where laughter lies,
In stillness, the spirit flies.

Time slows down in this retreat,
Where solitude and solace meet.
Reclusive thoughts find their heartbeat,
In this haven, swift and sweet.

Wrapped in comfort, we take flight,
Drifting through the velvet night.
A soft place, our souls ignite,
Embracing dreams in pure delight.

Quicksand of Wishes and Regrets

Wishes bloom like fragile flowers,
Entwined with time and fleeting hours.
Regrets linger, casting powers,
As we sink beneath their towers.

In the mire of hopes misplaced,
With every step, we lose our grace.
Choices made, a haunting trace,
Caught in the quicksand's cold embrace.

Yet from the depths, we learn to rise,
Through tangled dreams, we seek the skies.
In every stumble, wisdom lies,
The heart's desire never dies.

So take a breath, embrace the fall,
In quicksand's grasp, find strength in all.
For from these depths, we hear the call,
To rise again, and stand up tall.

Weaving Silk from Raw Threads

From humble strands, a tale begins,
Intertwined with hopes and sins.
With deft hands, we weave our skins,
Crafting dreams where life now spins.

Each thread a story, soft yet strong,
Knotted together where we belong.
In every pattern, a sacred song,
Echoes of the past, loud and long.

Colors bleed, a vibrant dance,
In the fabric of fate, we take a chance.
With every stitch, a second glance,
Embracing the unknown, we advance.

Silk emerges from chaos' breath,
A tapestry born from life and death.
Weaving journeys with every step,
In the loom of time, our hearts are kept.

Resilience Wrapped in Quietude

In the stillness, strength takes root,
Soft whispers of hope, a gentle suit.
Through trials faced, we rise anew,
Wrapped in the calm, we break on through.

With every dawn, a promise born,
In silent battles, courage worn.
Roots dig deep in fertile ground,
In quietude, our truth is found.

Beneath the weight of heavy skies,
The heart beats on, or it defies.
With every tear, a story told,
Resilience blooms, brave and bold.

So let the world in chaos spin,
For peace lives deep, it dwells within.
Through storms that rage, we find our way,
Wrapped in quietude, we shall stay.

Chasing the Light Behind Closed Eyes

In the depths where shadows play,
A flicker glows, it finds a way.
Behind the lids, a journey starts,
Chasing the light that fills our hearts.

Colors dance in vibrant dreams,
Echoes of hope in silvery beams.
Through whispers soft, the visions rise,
Infinite worlds behind closed eyes.

Darkness fades when we believe,
Each twinkling star, a chance to weave.
With courage found in gentle sighs,
We reach for light behind closed eyes.

Awake or lost in slumber's call,
The spirit soars, it breaks the fall.
In waking dreams, our souls will fly,
Chasing the light, we touch the sky.

Whirlwind of Everyday Wonders

In the rush of fleeting days,
Simple joys in secret ways.
A child's laugh, a soft embrace,
Life's small treasures we must trace.

The morning dew on blades of grass,
Moments lost, but memories pass.
In every breath, a chance to see,
The miracles that set us free.

Through crowded streets and buzzing sounds,
In laughter shared, joy abounds.
A whisper, a glance, all intertwine,
In the whirlwind, the heart can shine.

Let us not miss the beauty there,
In ordinary, the riches rare.
Amidst the chaos, we can find,
A whirlwind of wonders, life unconfined.

Heartbeats in a Crowded Room

In a sea of faces, hearts align,
Silent stories in every sign.
Among the chatter, a pulse we share,
Connections spark in the crowded air.

Eyes that meet, a fleeting glance,
In the rhythm of life, we dance.
With every heartbeat, a tale unfolds,
In crowded rooms, warmth over cold.

Laughter rises, a joyful sound,
In kindred spirits, love is found.
For though we're many, not alone,
Our heartbeats sing in rhythms grown.

So let the noise around us blend,
In every soul, a spark, a friend.
Together here, in this vast plume,
Our heartbeats thrive in the crowded room.

Melodies of the Unseen

Whispers dance on the evening breeze,
Notes of silence weave through the trees.
In shadows deep, a song takes flight,
Carried softly into the night.

Stars hum gently in the dark,
With every twinkle, they leave a mark.
Echoes linger in the heart's embrace,
Melodies hidden, time cannot erase.

A symphony born from dreams untold,
In quiet moments, secrets unfold.
Listen closely, let your spirit soar,
For unseen music is forevermore.

Colors of a Sullen Sky

Gray clouds gather, heavy with thought,
A canvas brushed with feelings fought.
Shades of blue in the shadows play,
While hope flickers, fading away.

Each drop of rain tells a tale deep,
Of long lost wishes we wish to keep.
In muted hues, the heart finds its song,
Yearning for brightness where we belong.

Streaks of orange in twilight glow,
Reminding us of moments we know.
Yet still the veil of sorrow plows,
Colors paint sorrow on silent brows.

A Journey Through My Inner Landscapes

Paths composed of winding thoughts,
Hills of dreams, battles fought.
Forests whisper with voices lost,
In echoes deep, I count the cost.

Meadows bloom with joyful light,
Where shadows cast in fleeting fright.
Rivers carve the soul's terrain,
A journey through joy, sorrow, and pain.

Mountains rise, relentless and bold,
Stories etched in moments told.
With every step, I redefine,
The landscapes within, truly mine.

Ripples of Uncertainty

Waves lap gently against the shore,
Echoes of questions, forevermore.
What lies hidden beneath the skin?
A tide of doubt, where dreams begin.

In still waters, the mind will race,
Trying to find some peaceful space.
Each ripple spreads through time and thought,
Leaving traces of battles fought.

Yet within the murky depths I find,
The strength of hope, intertwined.
For in uncertainty's tender embrace,
Lies the beauty of the human race.

Dances of Dissonance

In shadows cast by fading light,
Whispers rise that stir the night.
A melody of lost embrace,
Where silence finds its fractured space.

Rhythm clashes in a silent room,
Echoes skate on threads of gloom.
Yet in chaos, a spark ignites,
A dance unfolds with wild delights.

Steps unsteady, yet hearts align,
In the turmoil, we find the sign.
The dissonance a sweet refrain,
A harmony born from the pain.

Stories Untold

Pages torn from ancient lore,
Whispers held, but never more.
Faded ink and dreams that fade,
In the quiet, secrets wade.

Voices linger in the breeze,
Carrying tales that come with ease.
Sunset paints the sky with gold,
Yet within, a story's hold.

Between the lines, a truth will find,
Lessons learned, the past entwined.
In silence speaks the heart profound,
A journey waits, still yet unbound.

Beneath the Surface

Ripples dance on water's skin,
Stillness hides the depths within.
What lies under, dark and deep,
Secrets that the shadows keep.

Glimmers of life in twilight glow,
A hidden world, a gentle flow.
Tides that pull and hearts that yearn,
In quiet depths, we slowly learn.

Submerged thoughts in a tranquil sea,
Waves of dreams, they beckon me.
To dive deeper and find the pearl,
In unseen realms, our thoughts unfurl.

Notes from a Hidden Diary

In a corner where shadows dwell,
Lie the tales I've yet to tell.
A parchment worn with whispered fears,
Traces of laughter, echoes of tears.

Thoughts cascade like autumn leaves,
In ink, the heart quietly believes.
Each line a window to the soul,
In hidden notes, I find my whole.

A gentle pen that captures time,
Each scribble sings a silent rhyme.
In this diary where truths collide,
I unravel secrets I must confide.

In Pursuit of Fleeting Joys

In the morning's gentle glow,
I chase whispers on the breeze,
Children laughing, time moves slow,
Moments dance among the trees.

Sunsets painted hues so bright,
Fading slowly with the night,
Stars emerge to claim their place,
Silent dreams in their embrace.

Waves crash softly on the shore,
Each embrace, a fleeting score,
Life's a song of ebb and flow,
In pursuit of joys that glow.

Memories like fireflies weave,
Through the dark, we dare believe,
Chasing echoes, hearts in flight,
Fleeting joys that spark the night.

A Map of My Inner Universe

In caverns deep where shadows play,
Lie secrets waiting to be found,
Stars ignite in a vast array,
A universe within, profound.

Thoughts like comets streak the skies,
In orbits formed by dreams and fears,
Charting paths where wonder lies,
Echoes of forgotten years.

Galaxies of hopes reside,
Planets of love spin gently free,
Through the storms, my heart's the guide,
Navigating what's yet to be.

In the silence, answers bloom,
An atlas drawn by the mind's hand,
Mapping light amid the gloom,
A cosmos vast, a promised land.

The Light Woven Through Darkness

In the cloak of night's embrace,
Shadows linger, deep and wide,
Yet a spark finds its place,
Whispers of hope do abide.

Stars like stitches in the seam,
Threads of silver, weaving bright,
In the fabric of a dream,
Flickers dance, defying night.

Through the trials, courage grows,
Fires burn to guide the way,
In the dark, the spirit knows,
Light shall conquer, come what may.

From the depths, a voice will rise,
Shouting loud against despair,
For in each heart, a sun still lies,
Woven light is always there.

Treasures Hidden in Soft Glances

In the quiet spaces, we meet,
Where silence cradles heartbeats sweet.
A gaze exchanged, a story told,
In fleeting moments, treasures unfold.

Beneath the surface, secrets lie,
In every glance, a whispered sigh.
They shimmer softly, dusk to dawn,
The magic in the glances drawn.

Each sparkle brightens the mundane,
A simple glance, yet never plain.
Hidden gems in a world so vast,
These treasures linger, unsurpassed.

Let eyes converse, let spirits soar,
In soft glances, we find the core.
A language rich with love's intent,
In every look, our hearts are lent.

The Heart's Diary of Unwritten Verses

In the quiet of the night, I dream,
Pages blank, yet thoughts redeem.
Words unspoken, feelings deep,
Stories wrapped in secrets keep.

The ink of heart, it flows so slow,
With every pulse, new tales may grow.
A diary kept within my chest,
Where unwritten verses find their rest.

Each day a chapter, life unfolds,
But silent whispers never told.
I pen my hopes in shadows' light,
In the heart's diary, dark and bright.

Though words may falter, feelings soar,
In every beat, I long for more.
The tales of love, of joy, of pain,
In unwritten verses, I remain.

Flickering Flames of Emotion

In the heart's hearth, flames ignite,
Flickering shadows dance in the night.
Joy and sorrow burn so bright,
Each moment cherished, taken flight.

Emotions swirl like autumn leaves,
Catching light, each one deceives.
Yet in their glow, truth glimmers near,
A tapestry woven with joy and fear.

Each spark a memory, sharp and sweet,
A journey embarked, never complete.
Through flickers dim and fiery blaze,
Our hearts relay their wild displays.

In every flame, a story lies,
Stories told through laughter and sighs.
Though they may fade and dusk may fall,
The flickering flames unite us all.

In Between the Lines of Sorrow

Amidst the words, a silence vast,
In sorrow's grip, shadows are cast.
The lines unspoken, heavy weight,
In between them, we contemplate.

Each tear falls down like morning dew,
With every line, a hidden cue.
The pain that lingers, whispers low,
In the margins where feelings grow.

Through grief's embrace, we seek the light,
Between the lines, hope takes its flight.
A dance of sorrow, yet we find,
In between the lines, we're entwined.

Though shadows loom and hearts may ache,
In between the lines, we still wake.
Learning to breathe, to see the dawn,
Finding strength in the lines withdrawn.

Secrets Whispered in the Wind

In the stillness of the night,
Whispers float on gentle air,
Carrying tales of dreams forgotten,
Secrets linger, unaware.

Beneath the stars, they softly dance,
Leaves rustle, nature's voice,
Whispers weave through ancient trees,
Make us listen, make us choice.

Echoes of laughter, sighs of woe,
Stories wrapped in twilight's breath,
In every gust, a life untold,
A tapestry of love and death.

So close your eyes and feel the breeze,
Let the secrets find their way,
In the quiet, hear your heart,
As the wind begins to play.

Flickers of Light in the Dark

In the shadows where hope hides,
Flickers glimmer, faint but bright,
Stars appear, a cosmic dance,
Guiding us through the endless night.

Beneath the moon's soft silver glow,
Whispers of dreams begin to spark,
In every heart, a flicker glows,
Illuminating paths through dark.

Each tiny flame, a story told,
Breath of courage, tales of grace,
In the depths of despair's clutch,
Flickers rise, a warm embrace.

Together they burn, bright and bold,
A beacon for lost souls to find,
In darkness' grasp, we're never cold,
With flickers of light, we're intertwined.

A Tapestry of Human Experience

Threads of laughter, threads of tears,
Woven tightly in this life,
Colors bright, or dull with fears,
A tapestry of joy and strife.

Each moment stitched with care and dreams,
Every heart beats, a unique sound,
In this fabric, love redeems,
Connections made, are tightly bound.

Joy and sorrow, intertwined,
In every stitch, a story lives,
Through trials faced, wisdom finds,
A gift of empathy it gives.

So share your thread, let others know,
We're richer when we intertwine,
In this tapestry, we all grow,
Celebrating life, yours and mine.

Cracks in the Armor of Silence

In silence thick, truths lie hidden,
Cracks begin to form and quake,
Voices rise, once softly bidden,
Eager hearts begin to break.

In the quiet, shadows loom,
Secrets whisper, lost for years,
Amid the stillness, there's a boom,
A breaking free from frozen fears.

Words unspoken find their power,
In vulnerability, we dare,
No longer trapped by silent hours,
Our stories soar through open air.

So let the cracks in silence show,
The strength within our fragile skin,
In each unveiled truth, we grow,
Embracing light where once was sin.

Echoes of Emotion

In the silence, voices play,
Shadows dance, lost in sway.
Memories drape like old lace,
Time whispers soft, leaves no trace.

Tears like rain on gentle ground,
Fading echoes, a haunting sound.
Joy and sorrow intertwined,
In the heart, secrets confined.

Tides of Thoughts

Waves crash in, pulling tight,
Thoughts drift like stars at night.
Moments rise, then dip away,
A dance of dreams, come what may.

Currents rush, a wild stream,
In their depths, a fragile dream.
Tides pull back, revealing shores,
A canvas where the heart explores.

Fragments of My Heart

Splintered pieces scattered wide,
Each a tale, a feeling's guide.
Shards of laughter gently break,
In their midst, the echoes wake.

Beneath the pain, there's beauty too,
A tapestry of every hue.
With every crack, a story flows,
In fragments, love forever grows.

Whispers of the Mind

Thoughts that flutter, soft as wings,
Hidden truths that silence brings.
Mind's embrace, a tight cocoon,
Like shadows dancing 'neath the moon.

Echoes linger, softly sigh,
In the stillness, questions lie.
A soft murmur, fears unwind,
In quiet moments, peace we find.

Blossoms of Hope Amongst the Thorns

In the garden where shadows creep,
Blooms of courage, promises to keep.
Among the thorns that pierce the light,
Resilience grows, bold and bright.

Each petal tells a tale of grace,
In harshest times, they find their place.
With colors bold against the dark,
A testament, they leave their mark.

Through storms that howl and winds that sting,
These blossoms dance, and hope takes wing.
With every bloom, our dreams revive,
In thorny paths, we learn to thrive.

So here amidst the strife and pain,
Hope's gentle whispers will remain.
For in our hearts, the flowers grow,
A testament to strength, we know.

Reflections in a Broken Mirror

Cracks run deep in silver frames,
Scattered images, forgotten names.
Each shard reveals a life once whole,
Fragments whisper, echo the soul.

In pieces lie our tales untold,
The warmth of memories, once so bold.
A glimpse of joy, a shadowed fear,
Reflections dance, crystal clear.

Through shattered glass, we learn to see,
The beauty wrapped in fragility.
Each split and fracture serves a part,
To mend the seams, to heal the heart.

So gather shards beneath the light,
Create a mosaic from the night.
In every break, a story seeks,
To find its voice, the heart still speaks.

The Breath I Hold

In stillness, silence wraps the night,
A breath I hold, a whispered light.
Moments pause, the world slips away,
In this space, I long to stay.

Like fragile wings against the storm,
Each breath, a promise to transform.
I feel the pulse, the rhythm slow,
In the depths, my spirit grows.

Through every inhalation, I find,
The weight of worries left behind.
Exhale the doubts, release the chain,
In quietude, I rise again.

The breath I hold is life anew,
A chance to dream, to feel, to true.
In every sigh, a spark ignites,
The journey starts, my heart takes flight.

Fluctuations of an Untamed Spirit

Waves crash fiercely on the shore,
An untamed spirit yearning for more.
It dances wild, a vibrant flame,
Unchained from conformity's name.

Through valleys low and mountains high,
It seeks the stars, unafraid to fly.
With every rise and every fall,
The heart beats strong, it answers the call.

In every fluctuation, it learns to bend,
A restless soul, it will not end.
Like rivers flow, ever-changing course,
An essence free, it draws its force.

So let the winds of change arise,
Embrace the chaos, reach for the skies.
For in the flux, there lies the truth,
An untamed spirit, forever youth.

Threads of My Existence

In the fabric of the night, I weave,
Whispers of dreams that gently cleave.
Moments captured, fragile and bright,
Stitched together, a tapestry of light.

Echoes of laughter, shadows of tears,
Intertwined stories throughout the years.
Each thread a memory, vibrant, alive,
In this delicate dance, I learn to thrive.

Fears and hopes in every line,
A journey written, forever divine.
Stitched with love, endurance, and grace,
These threads of existence shape my place.

In the loom of time, I stand tall,
Embracing the weave, embracing it all.
Every stitch a testament to my heart,
In the threads of my existence, I partake in art.

Veils of Vibration

Softly they whisper, echoes in air,
Veils of vibration, a dance ever rare.
Silent melodies drift through the night,
Unseen rhythms, a gentle delight.

Crimson and azure, colors collide,
In this symphony, we softly glide.
Twinkling starlight plays on the strings,
Veils of vibration, the joy that it brings.

In the pulse of the universe's heart,
Each note a story, a brand new start.
Feeling the cadence, lost in the flow,
Veils of vibration, together we grow.

A tapestry of sounds, woven with care,
In every heartbeat, in every prayer.
Together we rise, forever entwined,
In the veils of vibration, love we find.

Fireflies in the Dark

In the still of the night, they softly glow,
Fireflies dancing, putting on a show.
A flicker of hope in shadows so deep,
Glimmers of magic that wake from their sleep.

Whispers of light, in fragile flights,
Guiding our dreams through the dark, starry nights.
Each tiny spark, a wish on its way,
Lighting the paths where our hearts wish to stay.

With wings made of stardust, they flit and sway,
Reminding us gently to cherish the play.
In moments of silence, they grace us with peace,
Fireflies in the dark, our worries release.

As they weave through the fog, a delicate trance,
We join in their waltz, lost in their dance.
With each fleeting glow, our spirits arise,
Fireflies in the dark, a celestial surprise.

Lullabies of Longing

Soft as the mist that blankets the dawn,
Lullabies of longing, a sweet, gentle yawn.
In the quietest hours, dreams start to hum,
Whispers of wishes, a comforting drum.

Like the tide that kisses the shore with care,
These lullabies linger, weaving through air.
Reciting the tales of what could have been,
In the cradle of night, where lost loves begin.

Every note sings of a heart held so tight,
Cradled in shadows, embraced by the night.
With each turn of the moon, desires take flight,
Lullabies of longing set the soul alight.

As dreams gently ripple and play on the breeze,
In the warmth of remembrance, we find our ease.
Through the depths of the night, these songs softly cling,
Lullabies of longing, forever they sing.

Harmonies of Hope

In the dawn's gentle light, we rise,
With whispers of dreams that fill the skies.
Hearts united, we stand so tall,
Together we hear hope's sweet call.

Through storms that may come, we won't despair,
For love and courage are always there.
Hand in hand, we face the day,
In the dance of life, we find our way.

With every note of joy we sing,
The world awakens, life takes wing.
In every chord, resilience gleams,
In the symphony of our shared dreams.

So let the melodies softly weave,
A tapestry of hope we believe.
Through every trial, through every fight,
Together we shine, a beacon of light.

Soliloquies of Solitude

In the silence, I find my voice,
Within the shadows, I make my choice.
Thoughts like echoes, softly tread,
In the crevices of my own head.

Each whisper lingers, a gentle sigh,
As night descends from a starry sky.
Time slows down, the world retreats,
In solitude, my heart still beats.

Alone yet whole, I wander deep,
Among the dreams, I silently keep.
A dance of thoughts, an endless stream,
In the lull of night, I find my dream.

These soliloquies, both fierce and kind,
A secret garden of my own mind.
In the quiet, I learn to see,
The beauty in my own company.

Ripples in a Quiet Sea

Beneath the surface, peace resides,
In the calm waves, my spirit glides.
The stillness whispers secrets old,
In the depths, treasures unfold.

Dancing softly, the ripples play,
Carried forth on a gentle sway.
Each wave a story, softly spun,
In the heart of the sea, we are one.

With every crest, a moment's grace,
Reflections shimmer, time and space.
In the quiet, I find my way,
Lost in the beauty of the day.

So let the tides embrace the shore,
In this tranquil place, I seek no more.
For in the ebb and flow we see,
The harmonious dance of you and me.

Lanterns on a Foggy Path

In the mist, the lanterns glow,
Guiding footsteps where few may go.
Softly glowing, they light the way,
Through the shrouded veil of gray.

Each flicker tells a tale untold,
Of dreams and journeys, brave and bold.
In the fog, we find our trust,
As shadows dance, and hopes adjust.

The path ahead may twist and turn,
But within each heart, a fire will burn.
With every step, we share the light,
Illuminating the depth of night.

So let us walk this journey long,
With lanterns bright and spirits strong.
Together we forge through time and haze,
Creating memories in the misty maze.

A Symphony of Sentiments

In whispers sweet, the night enfolds,
Emotions dance, like stories told.
Each note a brush, a gentle stroke,
Weaving dreams in silver smoke.

Hearts collide in rhythmic trace,
Echoing in this hallowed space.
Melodies weave through tender sighs,
As twilight hums beneath the skies.

Empty walls, they start to breathe,
In harmony where spirits weave.
As laughter swells and moments cling,
Together we flow, a song we sing.

Through vibrant chords, our spirits soar,
Each feeling drawn, forevermore.
Let symphonies of love unwind,
In every heartbeat, souls aligned.

Colors Beneath the Skin

Underneath the surface sheen,
A tapestry of hues unseen.
With every pulse, with every beat,
A canvas where our secrets meet.

Crimson joy and azure fear,
Emerald dreams that draw us near.
In shades of grief and golden glow,
A palette rich, a vibrant flow.

Brushstrokes of pain, caress of grace,
The colors shift, an endless chase.
In every tear and every grin,
The light reveals what's deep within.

From muted tones to bright display,
Our stories told in vibrant sway.
In this mosaic, hearts entwine,
Each shade a truth, uniquely mine.

Between Breath and Beat

In the stillness, life begins,
Between each breath, our moment spins.
A heartbeat echoes, soft and slow,
In this space, true feelings grow.

Time suspended, whispers flow,
A gentle comfort, soft and low.
In rhythm found, we touch the core,
What lies between, we can explore.

Every breath, a sacred vow,
In stillness, we unravel now.
Between the lines of love and fear,
Connection blooms when we draw near.

In silent pauses, we can trust,
Between the beats, it's love or rust.
Embrace the dance of quiet grace,
In every heartbeat, find your place.

Chasing Fleeting Moments

In shadows cast by fading light,
We chase the dreams that take their flight.
Through laughter's echo, whispers glide,
A fleeting touch, a swelling tide.

As sunset wraps the world in gold,
We capture stories, brave and bold.
In every glance, a spark ignites,
The fleeting hours, our hearts' delights.

Yet time, a thief that won't relent,
Steals precious seconds, seldom spent.
We grasp at hands, but they slip by,
Moments like clouds in the vast sky.

So let us dance, though time may flee,
In every heartbeat, find the key.
Through fleeting moments, love will grow,
For in this chase, true magic shows.

Uncertain Tides of Time

The waves they ebb and flow,
Carrying whispers of the past,
Footprints lost in shifting sands,
Moments fade, yet shadows cast.

Clouds drift by, unchained and free,
Sunrise heralds dreams anew,
Yet in the depths uncertainty,
Hides the truth we once just knew.

Seasons change, as leaves will fall,
Echoes linger on the breeze,
Time, a river broad and tall,
Washes hopes with gentle ease.

In the silence, hearts align,
Searching for what's left behind,
The tides will always shift in time,
But memories, they softly bind.

Chains of Thought and Freedom

In the recess of the mind,
Whispers clash, a stormy sea,
Thoughts like shadows intertwined,
Yearning for the chance to be.

Chains of doubt hold tight their reign,
Yet beneath, a spark ignites,
Craving space to break the chain,
To soar like birds in azure flights.

Voices nag, but dreams persist,
Calling forth from deep within,
Freedom hides, a tempting mist,
Waiting for the brave to win.

With each step, the shackles break,
In the light, we feel so bold,
From the past, we start to wake,
Embracing futures yet untold.

Echoing Laughter in Empty Spaces

In rooms where silence dwells alone,
A giggle echoes through the air,
Memories dance on walls of stone,
In the void, they linger and share.

Empty chairs hold whispered songs,
Faint melodies from times gone by,
Laughter weaves where all belongs,
Filling gaps where shadows lie.

In the corners, joy resides,
Waiting for a heart to find,
In hollow halls our laughter bides,
A testament to love entwined.

For every silence bears a trace,
Of moments bright, of love embraced,
Echoing laughter fills the space,
A reminder, we are interlaced.

A Symphony of Restless Affections

In twilight's haze, our hearts collide,
A cadence pulses through the night,
Melodies of longing glide,
In whispered words, we chase the light.

Each glance a note, a soft refrain,
Resonating in the air,
With every touch, we feel the gain,
Of love entwined, beyond compare.

Yet restless hearts can't stay confined,
They yearn to roam, to seek, to fly,
In symphonies, the lost we find,
Revelations in a sigh.

As stars align in cosmic dance,
Our spirits spin in vibrant hues,
A symphony of sweet romance,
Where every whisper feels like news.

Traces of Serenity in Chaos

In the storm, a whisper calls,
Softly pushing through the squalls.
Gentle light breaks through the gray,
Guiding us to find our way.

Among the rushing winds we stand,
Holding tightly to each hand.
Peace emerges from the fight,
Brightening the darkest night.

Footsteps falter, yet we tread,
Love's warm glow begets no dread.
In turmoil, we find our core,
Awakening to something more.

Beneath the chaos, calm will bloom,
A flower growing through the gloom.
Let the heart find its clear voice,
In upheaval, we rejoice.

Puzzles of the Heart Aligning

Pieces scattered, far and wide,
Searching for where they can reside.
In the chaos, whispers sing,
Connecting tales that love can bring.

Each fragment tells a sacred truth,
In the hues of our lost youth.
Fitting shapes, a dance divine,
Hearts entwined, the stars align.

Moments shared, like gentle streams,
Floating softly through our dreams.
With every glance, our souls ignite,
Painting shadows with pure light.

Trust the journey, trust the ride,
Love's a puzzle, hearts the guide.
In the stillness, we will find,
The sacred threads that bind mankind.

In the Garden of Emotional Echoes

Amidst the blooms, our secrets grow,
Silent whispers, soft and low.
Petals delicate, hearts exposed,
In this garden, truth unfolds.

Every echo holds a tale,
In the silence, we set sail.
Tendrils wrap around the past,
In this haven, peace will last.

Colors blend, like laughter shared,
In this space, we are bared.
Roots entwined in gentle grace,
Emotional echoes find their place.

Time does linger, love does grow,
Through the seasons, hearts will flow.
In this garden, safe and bright,
We find solace in the light.

Songs of Solitude

In the quiet, voices hum,
Echoes of what once was fun.
Notes of longing fill the air,
In solitude, we find our care.

Softly strumming on my heart,
Melodies that make me start.
In the stillness, I embrace,
The tender truth of my own space.

Waves of feelings crash and sway,
In the silence, I won't stray.
Finding rhythm in my plight,
Songs of solitude take flight.

Under stars, reflections glow,
Whispered secrets, soft and low.
In each pause, a chance to know,
The beauty found in being slow.

Clusters of Thoughts Unraveled

In the garden of my mind, thoughts bloom,
Whispers dance like petals, chasing gloom.
Threads entwined in colors, vivid and bright,
Fragments of dreams gleam in morning light.

Tangled ideas drift like autumn leaves,
Carried on winds, escaping their sheaves.
In silence, they gather, unsure and shy,
Waiting for the moment to take to the sky.

Beneath the branches, shadows play tricks,
Echoes of past visions, soft and mixed.
Each cluster a memory, woven tight,
Yearning for freedom, to soar into flight.

With each unravel, a story unfolds,
Secrets come alive, the heart gently scrolled.
In this quiet chaos, I seek to find,
The beauty within, in clusters entwined.

Footprints in the Sands of Time

Along the shore, where dreams once walked,
Footprints marked tales, in whispers they talked.
The tide rolls in, with each break and swell,
Cleansing the traces, yet stories still dwell.

Each step a memory, etched in the sand,
Moments of laughter, of love gently planned.
The sun dips low, in hues of gold,
A canvas of echoes, of stories retold.

Waves crash gently, erasing the past,
Yet the heart holds tight to shadows that last.
With every footprint, a journey unfolds,
In the sands of time, life's warmth it holds.

Beneath the stars, I walk once again,
In search of those footprints, where love has lain.
Though the ocean may wash them far and wide,
In the heart's deepest chamber, they still reside.

Waves Crash Against Silent Shores

The ocean roars, its voice wild and free,
Waves crash like thunder, set spirits at sea.
Amidst the chaos, a calm does await,
Silent shores whisper, they beckon my fate.

Glimmers of silver, where water meets land,
Secrets are spoken, unplanned and unplanned.
Each wave a heartbeat, a pulse of life's song,
Carrying tales where the souls all belong.

From depths of the ocean, dreams drift and rise,
In swirling currents, the soul learns to fly.
Against the stillness, a tempest does roar,
Yet silence embraces what waves can't explore.

Here by the water, I learn to endure,
Finding the strength in the gentle and pure.
For in every crash, there's a story untold,
A rhythm of life, in the ocean's bold hold.

Muffled Cries of Lost Aspirations

In shadows they linger, those hopes held tight,
Muffled cries echo, fading from sight.
Whispers of dreams that once danced in the air,
Now sigh in silence, lost in despair.

With every heartbeat, a wish slips away,
Fading like sunlight at the end of the day.
Each aspiration wrapped in layers of doubt,
Flickers of longing, learning to shout.

Yet deep in the silence, a spark still remains,
A flicker of courage that quietly gains.
For within every heart, lies a fire aglow,
Waiting for moments when dreams dare to flow.

Though shadows may hover, and fears may entwine,
Lost aspirations still yearn to align.
In the depths of the silence, they quietly rise,
Muffled no longer, they reach for the skies.

A Palette of Unspoken Emotions

Colors swirl in silent plea,
Beneath the surface, truth we see.
Brushes dip in shades of pain,
Hues of joy in quiet rain.

Whispers echo in the night,
Each stroke reveals the hidden fright.
Vibrant strokes of laughter flit,
In every shade, the heart must sit.

Moments brush against the soul,
A canvas rich, yet still so whole.
Between the lines, a story sleeps,
In every hue, a secret keeps.

In this gallery of the heart,
We find the beauty in the art.
Unseen emotions mingle here,
A palette bright, yet woven with fear.

Threads of Joy and Sorrow

Two threads wove in life's vast loom,
Joy's bright whispers, sorrow's gloom.
In every stitch, a tale unfolds,
Of laughter shared and moments cold.

Vibrant colors dance in light,
While shadows linger in the night.
Each twist and turn, a choice we make,
For every smile, a heart might ache.

Weaving memories through the years,
Each fiber soaked in hopes and fears.
A tapestry of hearts entwined,
In joy and sorrow, peace we find.

As threads connect, we come to see,
The beauty in our tapestry.
In every strain, a lesson grows,
In joy and pain, our spirit flows.

Dancing Shadows in the Mind's Corner

Shadows waltz where thoughts collide,
In corners dark where dreams abide.
A flicker here, a shadow there,
Whispers swirl in the midnight air.

Ghostly forms in silent grace,
Echoes of a familiar face.
They twist and turn, a fleeting sight,
In the recesses of the night.

Each shadow tells a story missed,
Of gentle moments, love's soft kiss.
Dancing lightly, they drift away,
But in our hearts, they'll always stay.

In the mind's corner, secrets weave,
Where shadows dance, we still believe.
In every flicker, life remains,
A silent rhythm in our veins.

The Weight of Unshed Tears

Heavy hearts bear silent cries,
In whispered sorrows, pain complies.
Each tear unshed, a weight to hold,
A story aching to be told.

In shadows deep, emotions swell,
Silent echoes, a heart's farewell.
Beneath the surface, struggles lie,
In every glance, a muted sigh.

A burden carried, not in sight,
Yet overwhelming in the night.
Through clenched fists, our spirits strain,
The weight of tears, a quiet pain.

Yet through the sorrow, strength may bloom,
Hope finds light amid the gloom.
In every drop, a seed may grow,
From unshed tears, the soul will glow.

Cascade of Heartbeats

In twilight's embrace, we softly sway,
Echoes of laughter drift into the fray.
A cascade of moments, fleeting and bright,
Pulsing like stars in the blanket of night.

With every heartbeat, we dance on the breeze,
Wrapped in the whispers of rustling trees.
Together we create a symphony fine,
A rhythm of love that forever will shine.

The mountains bear witness, the rivers sing low,
As we carve our path through the ebb and the flow.
In this cascade of heartbeats, we find our song,
Together, forever, where we both belong.

So let us keep dancing, just you and I,
Beneath the vast canvas of twilight's soft sky.
With each passing moment, let's cherish the art,
Of love's gentle rhythm, the pulse of the heart.

Reflections in a Still Pond

Beneath the moonlight, a mirror unfolds,
Secrets of nature in watery holds.
Trees sway like dancers, their shadows aligned,
Each ripple a story, each wave intertwined.

The echoes of whispers, the songs of the night,
Glimmers of silver, a soft, guiding light.
In this stillness, I find my own voice,
Reflections of memory merge with my choice.

A world dipped in silence, where thoughts can roam free,
In the embrace of the water, I am simply me.
The stars gently tremble, their beauty laid bare,
In reflections that shimmer, I breathe in the air.

So let me be still as the night carries on,
In the heart of the moment, my fears gently yawn.
With every bright flicker, a promise I make,
To cherish these echoes, for love's endless sake.

Journey through Inner Landscapes

Through valleys of thought, my spirit will roam,
In landscapes of yearning, I carve out a home.
Mountains of doubt rise, yet valleys provide,
A journey unending, where dreams will abide.

Each step tells a story, each breath brings a hue,
In meadows of colors, both vivid and true.
The whispers of wisdom flow soft like a stream,
Guiding the heart toward the light of a dream.

With shadows of struggle, I rise and I fall,
In the depths of despair, I hear nature's call.
The winds of resilience carry me far,
As I navigate pathways beneath the North Star.

So here on this journey, through wild, untamed space,
I discover the beauty in every trace.
In the realms of the inner, my spirit takes flight,
Forever unfolding, in love's endless light.

Unraveled Tapestries

Threads of connection weave stories untold,
In the fabric of life, both fragile and bold.
Colors, they swirl in a dance of the past,
Each knot reveals moments that ever will last.

From hearts that entwined in the warmth of the day,
To shadows of silence where dreams slipped away.
Unraveled, unruly, yet still beautifully spun,
Every flaw and each crease tells of battles we've won.

Patterns emerge in the warmth of the light,
Sewn with compassion through the long, starry night.
With laughter and sorrow, all threads play their part,
In the tapestry held close, stitched deep in the heart.

So cherish the fabric, both worn and refreshed,
It weaves our existence, forever enmeshed.
In the gallery of life, let our stories unfold,
As the unraveled becomes a tapestry bold.

Mirror of My Mood

In the glass, reflections fall,
Each twist revealing all.
Hope dances in the light,
Heart's whispers take flight.

Fleeting shadows play their game,
Courage hides, but it's not to blame.
Emotions surge like tides,
In silence, my truth abides.

Colors change with every breath,
Life and dreams entwined in depth.
Joy and sorrow blend and fuse,
In this mirror, I choose to lose.

Every smile, every tear,
Reflects the dreams I hold dear.
A symphony of silent sighs,
In the mirror, my spirit flies.

Waves of Silent Yearning

On the shore, the ocean calls,
Whispers echo in the halls.
Each wave a tale to unfold,
Of hopes and dreams yet untold.

Moonlit nights sail on the breeze,
Carrying wishes with such ease.
Hearts adrift in endless seas,
Finding peace in gentle pleas.

Dancing ripples, soft and light,
Guide my thoughts into the night.
Tides of longing, soft and slow,
Cradle secrets no one knows.

In the depths, the silence stirs,
With every pulse, the ocean purrs.
Yearning flows with each heartbeat's tease,
In the waves, my soul finds ease.

Canvas of My Soul

Brushstrokes merge on empty white,
Colors bleed into the night.
Every hue a piece of me,
Captured in this artful spree.

Shapes of joy and strains of pain,
Layered deep like summer rain.
Dreams take flight on vibrant wings,
In this canvas, my heart sings.

Textures blend in soft embrace,
A tapestry of time and space.
Every line tells tales of old,
A story painted, brave and bold.

In the quiet, colors hum,
Echoes of what's yet to come.
Each creation, a fleeting glance,
On this canvas, I take my chance.

Shadows of Unspoken Words

In the dark, where secrets lie,
Silent thoughts begin to fly.
Every whisper held at bay,
In the shadows, they will stay.

Eyes that meet but do not speak,
In those moments, hearts grow weak.
Language lost in fleeting glances,
Unrevealed are all the chances.

Between the lines, a world concealed,
Every truth remains unsealed.
Yet within this quiet space,
Lives the hope, a warm embrace.

May the shadows find their light,
Turning whispers into flight.
Let the silence find its voice,
Shatter shadows, make a choice.

A Bouquet of Sentiments

In gardens lush with blooms so bright,
Each petal whispers soft delight.
A blend of love, both old and new,
A fragrant blend, just me and you.

Together we weave a tapestry,
Of memories sweet, wild and free.
The colors swirl, a vivid dance,
In every glance, a fleeting chance.

Beneath the stars, our secrets shared,
In every bud, a heart laid bare.
A bouquet rich with tender ties,
Together we bloom beneath the skies.

So hand in hand, let's walk this way,
In every bloom, our love's bouquet.
Through storms and sun, we will survive,
In this bouquet, our love alive.

Moonlight on My Heart

Moonlight drapes the silent night,
Softly whispering, pure and bright.
It dances lightly on my skin,
A gentle touch where dreams begin.

Each silver ray calls out your name,
Wrapped in shadows, still the same.
A tender glow, it lights the dark,
In every flicker lies a spark.

With every sigh, the stars align,
Their glow a promise, yours and mine.
In moonlit dreams, our spirits soar,
Forever bound, we seek for more.

So let the night embrace our fate,
In moonlight's arms, we truly wait.
To find in darkness, love's sweet art,
Together always, heart to heart.

Sunlight Through Shattered Glass

Sunlight filters, soft and warm,
Through fragments caught, a quiet charm.
Each shard reflects a moment bright,
In colors bold, dispelling night.

Across the floor, a scattered dream,
In every piece, a glimmered gleam.
The past, though cracked, beams with hope,
In shattered forms, we learn to cope.

As shadows stretch and dance away,
New patterns form with each new day.
A rainbow blooms in broken space,
In every flaw, a touch of grace.

So let the light weave through the pain,
In every crack, a love remains.
For through the shards, we see the whole,
With sunlight's guide, we find our soul.

Echoes of My Heart's Whispers

In quiet moments, softly heard,
The whispers drift, a gentle word.
Each echo carries dreams untold,
In shadows cast, our spirits bold.

Through valleys deep and mountains high,
Our hearts converse as time slips by.
In every thrum, a tale unfolds,
Each longing sigh, a heart that holds.

With every beat, memories rise,
In timeless dance beneath the skies.
The echoes weave a fabric fine,
Of love endured, of yours and mine.

In silent breezes, secrets pass,
Embracing time like fragile glass.
So let the echoes sing their song,
In heartbeats true, where we belong.

The Silent Symphony Within

In whispers soft, the echoes play,
A hidden tune, where shadows sway.
Each note a thought, a breath, a sigh,
In silence deep, our spirits fly.

The heartbeats pulse, a gentle song,
In solitude, where dreams belong.
The rhythm flows, an unseen stream,
With every beat, we chase the dream.

Beyond the noise, the calm resides,
A quiet space where love abides.
In stillness found, our souls align,
The silent symphony divine.

In every pause, a voice is heard,
In silent dreams, the soul's a bird.
With every rise, and every fall,
The silent symphony, it calls.

Fragments of a Dreamer's Soul

Scattered petals on the ground,
In gentle winds, their whispers sound.
Each fragment tells a tale so bright,
Of dreams that dance in morning light.

A wanderer's heart, forever torn,
In twilight's glow, a new day born.
Each shard reflects a vibrant hue,
A glimpse of paths that once we knew.

Through tangled threads, our stories merge,
In every loss, new hopes emerge.
Within the chaos, beauty lies,
In every tear, a star that cries.

A patchwork quilt of love and fears,
Stitched together by endless years.
In fragments found, the seeker whole,
The journey weaves a dreamer's soul.

Mosaic of Heartstrings

In colors bright, the heartstrings hum,
A vibrant tune where feelings come.
Each piece a pulse, each shade a thought,
In harmony, our lives are caught.

Fragments joined from different days,
A tapestry of joyful ways.
In laughter shared, in sorrow bled,
The mosaic glows where love has led.

With every line, a story weaves,
In every heart, a hope believes.
In silence soft, the strings will play,
A melody that lights the way.

Together here, our spirits dance,
In woven dreams, in every chance.
The mosaic sings, a heartfelt song,
In unity, where we belong.

When Words Are Too Heavy

In silence deep, the pain does sit,
Where heavy thoughts refuse to quit.
Each word, a weight, too hard to bear,
In quiet moments, we're laid bare.

The eyes may speak what lips can't find,
A language soft, a touch defined.
In every glance, the truth reveals,
A heart exposed, its secret feels.

When burdens swell and hearts must hide,
In shadows cast, we seek to glide.
With knowing sighs, we find the way,
To share our fears without the fray.

When words elude, let silence reign,
In every pause, we feel the pain.
For when the world feels far and wide,
In gentle stillness, souls confide.